WILD Animals

Lions, Tigers, Bears, & More!

Carus Publishing Company
Peterborough, NH
www.cricketmag.com

Staff
Editorial Director: Lou Waryncia
Project Editor: Charles Baker III
Designer: Brenda Ellis, Graphic Sense
Proofreader: Eileen Terrill

Text Credits
The content of this volume is derived from articles that first appeared in *CLICK*® magazine.
Contributors: Mary Ann Fraser ("How Animals Find Food"), Bertsy James ("Tata's Coyotes"),
Catherine Ripley ("Caribou Crossing" and "Safety in Numbers"); Buffy Silverman ("Pouch Life").

Picture Credits
Dynamic Graphics: 4, 10–13, 15; Photos.com: 5, 28; Mary Ann Fraser: 6–9; Picture Quest: 14;
Visuals Unlimited: 16–17, 20–21; Australian Tourist Board: 19; Betsy James: 22–27.

Cover
Dynamic Graphics

The Library of Congress Cataloging-in-Publication Data for *Wild Animals* is available at
http://catalog.loc.gov.

Carus Publishing
30 Grove Street, Peterborough, NH 03458
www.cricketmag.com

Printed in China

Table of Contents

Different Ways of Living

Some animals live in families. Some live in great big groups. And others live mostly by themselves. Animals have to find the right way of living together so they can stay safe, take care of their babies, and find food.

A giant panda mainly eats bamboo, and it takes lots of bamboo to fill up a panda! To make sure there's enough bamboo for everyone, each panda has a territory where it lives alone, except during mating time or when a mother is rearing her cub.

Some Animals Live Alone

Tigers are stealthy hunters who sneak up on prey such as deer or wild pigs — then pounce! But hunting is hard. It can take 10 tries before a tiger nabs a meal. Living alone means there's enough prey to eat and makes quiet hunting easier.

Lions are hunters, too. But they live in groups called prides. On the African plains, finding enough wildebeest, zebra, and antelope to eat is no problem. But catching them is. Lions have better luck when they hunt together, surrounding a herd and then flushing out their prey.

Others Like a Little Company

Eagles live and hunt together in lifelong pairs. A male and female help each other build a nest of sticks and twigs. When the eggs hatch, one parent stays home to protect the young eaglets, while the other searches for mice or fish to eat.

5

How Animals Find Food

All animals need to eat. Food gives them energy to grow, build homes, raise babies, and protect against danger. But each animal has its own kind of food and special way of finding it.

Some animals eat only plants, fruits, or seeds. They're called herbivores.

Giraffes eat mostly leaves. With their long necks and tongues, they reach high up into the trees.

Cows, zebras, tortoises, and kangaroos are grazers. They eat grasses and other plants low to the ground.

Animals that eat other animals are called carnivores.

A fox is a carnivore. It must move quickly and make sharp turns to catch the mice and other small animals it hunts.

Condors are scavengers. They eat the remains of animals killed by other carnivores. They like leftovers.

Animals that eat both plants and animals are called omnivores. Black bears eat whatever they can find during the different seasons of the year, including berries, fish, mushrooms, birds, small rodents, and insects. Having a lot of things they like to eat helps them get enough food.

Plant eaters, meat eaters, and scavengers are parts of a food chain. Gnus graze for grasses. A pack of hyenas kills and eats a gnu. And vultures eat the remains of the gnu that the hyenas leave behind. The food chain is nature's way of giving each animal the energy it needs.

Sometimes you can tell how an animal gets its food just by looking at it. Many carnivores have knifelike claws and teeth to catch their food. Tigers use their long claws and sharp teeth to both catch a deer and eat it.

Bird beaks come in many shapes and sizes. A pelican's bill scoops up fish out of the water. An eagle's beak tears meat into pieces small enough to swallow. A woodpecker's beak chips away at wood to make holes to store acorns, seek insects, or suck out sap.

Chameleons move very slowly, but their tongues are very fast. Their bodies change color, helping them blend into their surroundings. When an insect comes close, the chameleon shoots out its long, sticky tongue and pulls the insect into its mouth. GULP!

Often animals that live together work together to get food. A pod of humpback whales blows a net of bubbles to drive a school of fish close together. Then the whales swim through the fish, swallowing many at a time.

What animals eat determines how they look and how and where they live. Koalas are picky eaters. They eat only eucalyptus leaves, so they live in forests of eucalyptus trees in Australia.

But raccoons will eat whatever they can find. They live in forests, along streams, or even in your backyard.

Some animals are hunters, and some are hunted. Some even know clever tricks. Floating on its back, a sea otter opens a mussel shell by smashing it against a flat stone on its chest.

But every animal, everywhere, eats.

Did you know?
Koalas are not bears. They are marsupials, which means that they carry their young in a pouch like kangaroos.

Fight or Flight

On the plains of Africa, a lion is hunting a zebra. The lion is very powerful and has long, sharp claws. It fears no enemy. But it must eat to survive. The zebra cannot fight the lion, but it has other ways to stay safe. As the zebras graze, at least one member of the herd is alert for danger at all times. On the open, treeless plains, the zebras cannot hide from the lion. But it is hard for the lion to sneak up on the zebras, too.

A zebra can twist its big ears in almost any direction to listen to suspicious sounds. Its eyes are set high and on the sides of its head. It can see over the tall grass even when it is bending down to graze. And it can see not only what is in front of it, but also any danger that might be creeping up from the sides or even from behind.

The lion attacks suddenly with a tremendous burst of speed. Lions are quick, but zebras are fast, too. The zebra has long legs and can take big strides. Unless the zebra is old or the lion catches it by surprise, the zebra can usually outrun the lion.

Today, the zebra escapes, and the lion must hunt again.

Safety in Numbers

Finding a meerkat alone is unusual. Meerkats usually come in a bunch! That's because a meerkat stays safe by sticking close to its "mob," or group, of 10 to 25 meerkats.

As a meerkat hunts for food, it listens to the mob's chitter-chatter. Any alarm calls? Nope? Good, it can keep on digging. Sniff! Sniff! Any meerkat strangers about? Nope? Great, it can catch that cricket. Hey! That's a scorpion! The meerkat quickly bites off the poisonous stinger in the scorpion's tail. Then, it can enjoy a meal.

Within its home territory in the southern African desert, a mob can have four to five underground homes that help protect the animals from the extreme heat and cold. On freezing winter nights, the group huddles together deep underground to stay warm. In summer, overheating is a danger, and then meerkats spread out in their cool burrows.

Mother meerkats call on other adults to keep their pups safe. When Mom goes hunting for insects and worms, the pup-sitters are in charge. All adults help teach the pups how to hunt for food, fight, and look out for enemies.

Staying safe is easier with a guard on duty. Like all meerkats, the guard has excellent sight. The dark bands around its eyes cut down on the sun's glare. The guard scans the desert. It looks up and sees danger. Uh-oh! An eagle! The guard yowls. All the meerkats dive underground. If there are no holes or thorny bushes nearby, the meerkats lie still as can be.

Uh-oh, the guard barks. The bark, instead of a yowl, tells the mob that a jackal is near. This time the meerkats band together. They fluff out their fur, jump up and down, and make a lot of noise. Will the jackal leave them alone?

On its own, a meerkat makes an easy victim for many stronger animals. With its mob, the meerkat has a good chance of staying safe and ALIVE!

Galapagos Islands

They were once called the Enchanted Isles. The way they appeared and disappeared in the fog made early sailors think the islands might be floating in air. Strong ocean currents made sailing near them dangerous. And when sailors did manage to come ashore, they found marvelous plants and animals that lived nowhere else on earth.

Today, we call them the Galapagos Islands. Not many people live on the Galapagos. There isn't enough fresh water for them to drink. So, for all these years, plants and animals have thrived, undisturbed by humans. Today, scientists from around the world come to the Galapagos to study. They have learned a lot about how plants and animals grow and change in different environments.

Galapagos means "tortoise" in Spanish. And giant tortoises are probably the most famous animals on the islands. They can grow to be almost five feet tall and weigh 600 pounds! Scientists think that long ago there was probably only one kind of tortoise on the islands. Today, there are ten kinds, but they all fall into two basic groups. Each is specially suited for the landscape in which it lives.

The Galapagos are also home to two kinds of lizards that live nowhere else on earth. Land iguanas thrive on the hot, dry lava landscapes away from the shoreline. Their favorite food is cactus — which also thrives on hot, dry islands!

Marine iguanas are the only lizards in the world that swim and dive for food. They have flatter tails to help them swim better, and flatter noses to help them reach the algae they love. And the white stuff on their heads? Sea salt they've sneezed out!

Cormorants first flew to the Galapagos millions of years ago, on big, strong wings. But there were no enemies to fly away from on the islands, and all the fish they could eat were just offshore. Over many thousands of years, the cormorants' wings grew small and weak. Today, Galapagos flightless cormorants can no longer fly — but they are excellent divers!

Galapagos swallow-tailed gulls have red-rimmed eyes that glow in the dark and make them the only gulls that can see at night. Millions of years ago, these gulls hunted during the day. But frigate birds — bigger and meaner — kept stealing the fish right out of the gulls' beaks. Today, the gulls hunt at night — when the frigate birds don't bother them. The white spot on a gull's beak makes it easier for its chicks to see the beak and feed in the dark.

Did you know?

The Galapagos Islands include 125 land masses, but only 19 are large enough to be called islands. They are in the Pacific Ocean off the coast of South America and belong to the country of Ecuador. Only 20,000 people live on them.

Pouch Life

When you were born, you were very small. But you were not as tiny as a baby kangaroo. At birth, a baby gray kangaroo, called a joey, is the size of a jellybean.

A newborn joey has no hair and cannot see. But it can crawl. After it is born, it tears its way out of its birth sac. Then, it climbs up its mother's furry belly. Three minutes after it starts climbing, the pink baby reaches its mother's pouch and slips inside.

There, the joey sniffs and feels to find a nipple. For the next few months, it stays attached to the nipple, drinking its mother's milk and growing. While a joey is in the pouch, its mother sticks her head inside to lick her baby clean.

When it is about six months old, the joey wriggles and turns and pokes its head outside. Now its eyes are open, and hair is growing on its body.

A few months later, the joey is big enough to leave the pouch for the first time. Mother kangaroo

Go faster, Mom!

releases her pouch muscles, and the joey falls out. Sometimes a joey tumbles out when it stretches to pick grass. After a minute of standing on wobbly legs, the joey puts its head back in the pouch. The mother bends forward, and the joey kicks with its hind legs to somersault inside.

As the joey grows, it spends more time out of the pouch. It hops a few feet from its mother but soon returns. Occasionally, Mother kangaroo hops away. Then she stops and lets her joey catch up, teaching the joey to follow her.

Around its first birthday, a joey leaves the pouch for good. But it stays near its mother, and pokes its head into her pouch to drink milk. By then, there may be another tiny joey growing in the pouch.

The joey wanders a short distance away to eat grass. But even after the joey stops drinking milk, it follows Mother kangaroo and rests with her. If there is a danger, Mom calls with a click, and the joey hops back to be safe near its mother.

Caribou Crossing

I t's July, and way up north at the edge of the Arctic Ocean, on a treeless plain called the tundra, thousands and thousands of caribou are slowly munching and moving, moving and munching.

The caribou have traveled a long way from the spruce forests farther south where they spent the winter. Between April and June they trekked 300 miles — through melting springtime snow, across rivers, and up steep slopes — along trails that they've followed for hundreds of years.

This far north, the sun never sets during the summer, so there is no nighttime. Shrubs and grasses grow quickly in the endless sunshine. They make good munching for the mothers who are nursing hungry newborns.

The mothers keep watch for grizzly bears and golden eagles, which hunt newborns. And, every year, zillions of mosquitoes and flies come

to torment the caribou. Then the caribou seek the cool ocean breezes that will blow away the bugs.

Summer does not last long. One day in August there is a nip in the air, and the caribou know it's time to return to the spruce forests. They cannot stay on the tundra. In the winter, fierce, cold winds turn the snow as hard as cement — too hard for the caribou to dig under to find food.

By December, it is dark both day and night in the forests. As winter storms come and go, the caribou travel little. Their thick coats keep them warm. The caribou use their hooves like shovels to dig under the soft snow for plants called lichens, their winter food.

The winter is long, and finding enough to eat is not easy. One day in late March, a warm breeze blows. The snow is melting. The pregnant cows sense it is time to head north again to the tundra, where they will give birth in the summer. Off they go, one by one, walking single file. Several weeks later, the bulls follow. Once more, thousands of caribou are on the move.

Tata's Coyotes

I thought I heard ghosts crying outside in Tata's orchard. Mama came in all sleepy and hugged me in my quilt. "It's just coyotes, Ana."

"Yip-yip yaooo, yap-yap!" sounded the howls.

"Are they dogs?" I asked. I felt safe, now that she was there.

"Wild dogs. They live in the desert and the woods, but sometimes they come close to the house and sing."

Outside my window, the apricot trees bloomed white in the dark. Two bushy-tailed shadows flicked out of sight.

"Maybe they like apricots," I said. "Like me."

"Then they'll have to wait a month or two," said Mama, kissing me back to bed. "Like you."

"Coyotes like Tata's apricots," I told Papa at breakfast.

"I do, too. And last year's jam is almost gone." He licked his fingers. "I heard those coyotes. How times change! Tata would have shot them."

"Shot them!" Tata was my grandpa. He planted those trees. Why would he shoot singing dogs?

"Tata raised sheep. Coyotes sometimes killed his lambs to feed their pups. Everybody's got to eat," said Papa, "but mostly coyotes eat mice."

"Yay, coyotes!" said Mama. She hates mice.

"And frogs and snakes," Papa added.

"Yuck!" I cried. "Coyotes eat snakes?"

"They get desperate," he said, "when they can't get apricot jam."

It bothered me that Tata would shoot coyotes. But it bothered me that coyotes would kill lambs, too. Even to feed their pups. I was glad there weren't any lambs around.

The next evening, Papa came in smiling and said, "Can you be quiet, Ana? I've got a surprise."

We walked far along the irrigation ditch in the cold spring dusk and peeked through the willows. Papa whispered,

"See that hole under the cottonwood root?"

It was hard to see. Then, out of the hole crept a coyote, so nearly the color of the ground that it was almost invisible. It looked around, shook itself, and ran into the woods.

"There'll be pups in that den," Papa said, after we had tiptoed back to the orchard.

"Are they warm enough?"

"Coyotes dig cozy dens." He looked up at the apricot trees. "It's these blossoms that better stay warm, or no jam."

"Then we'd have to eat snakes," I said.

But the weather stayed warm, and the blossoms turned into a thousand baby apricots. Papa said the pups would be big enough to play outside the den.

"Let's go see!" I cried.

But he said no — if the parents got even a sniff of us, they'd move to a different place. "And it's not just people they have to watch out for. A hawk or an owl can carry off a pup, easy."

Then one day, Papa

brought home a brand-new pair
of binoculars.

We didn't go near the den. Instead
we climbed a faraway tree. Through the
binoculars, I saw a furry little face poke
out of the dark den. Then another, and
another. Four fat pups spilled out,
biting and wrestling. Their mama —
or maybe it was their papa — watched
over them.

"When the parents go hunting, they
chew up whatever they catch," Papa
whispered. "Then, they spit it up for
the pups to eat."

"Spit-up mice for breakfast? No way!"
I whispered back. "Papa, have you been
watching them all this time?"

"Not from close by. I didn't want to scare them." He laughed
softly. "Now, if Tata could hear me say that!"

The days got hot, and the apricots got ripe. Mama made
apricot jam, apricot pie, and apricot bread. She gave apricots to
all the neighbors, and there were still so many that they littered
the ground.

"Somebody needs to eat these apricots!" she said.

"Somebody is." Papa showed us coyote droppings in the
orchard — full of apricot pits!

Mama said, "I hope they're leaving room to eat mice."

We watched the pups grow bigger. At first, there were four of them. But one day, there were three, and by the end of the summer, only two.

"Where are the others?" I asked. But I knew.

Papa sighed. "No matter how hard the parents try to keep their babies safe, the hawks and owls grab some. As I said . . ."

I nodded. "Everybody's got to eat."

But I felt terrible. That night it got cold. I could hear owls calling in the dark trees, "Hu-huu!"

I scooted down in my quilt, like a coyote pup diving into its den. What if an owl swooped through my window? What if a hawk dove down?

Then I heard it: "Yip-yaoo, yap-yap!"

Something was different. Along with the grown-up voices in the orchard there were two new, high, squeaky ones.

"Yip-yip yaooo, squeak-squeak!"

I sat up in bed and laughed.

"Squeak-squeak!" It was as if each little coyote were singing, "So what if the world is full of owls? I can take care of myself now. Hear me sing!"

I went to the window and leaned out. Wind rustled the apricot leaves.

"I heard somebody's bare feet," Papa said behind me. "You OK, sweetheart?"

"The pups are singing!" I said. Together, we leaned and listened. "Yip-yaooo-squeak!"

"What would Tata do if he knew his orchard was a safe place for coyotes?" I asked.

Papa kissed my ear. "He'd shake his head and laugh."

27

Animal Eyes

It's hot in Africa! So a hippo spends most of its day in a cool lake or river. A hippo's eyes are in bumps on top of its head so it can see above the water while it swims along.

The eyes of a rhinoceros are on the sides of its head. That's good for seeing left and right, but how does a rhino see something straight in front? It turns its head from side to side and looks out of one eye at a time.

Can your eyes look in two directions at once? A chameleon's eyes can. While one eye searches for something to eat the other looks up, down, and all around, watching out for danger.

Glossary

Algae: a form of plant life that floats on water but does not have roots, stems or leaves and serves as food for some animals.

Carnivore: animals that eat other animals.

Environments: surroundings.

Herbivore: animals that eat only plants, fruit, or seeds.

Irrigation: to supply dry land with water using ditches.

Marine: of or relating to the sea or ocean.

Omnivore: animals that eat both plants and other animals.

Scavenger: an animal that feeds on dead or decaying plants or animals.

Stealthy: acting with quiet caution to avoid notice.

Strides: leaps and bounds.

Suspicious: distrustful.

Thrive: to do well.

Carnivore

Herbivore

Omnivore

Scavenger

North
America

Atlantic
Ocean

Ecuador

South
America

Galapagos
Islands

Pacific
Ocean

N
W   E
S

Arctic Ocean

Arctic Circle

Europe

Asia

Africa

Indian

Ocean

Australia

Antarctica

31

Animals are Amazing!

All around the world, animals roam on the earth, in the sky, and under the water. Come explore the fascinating world of animals through a unique collection of stories inspired from the pages of *CLICK*® magazine. Travel with us as we meet many types of animals and discover all the amazing ways they enhance our world.

$17⁹⁵ each

**Titles in the
Animal Series**

BUGS

PETS

WATER ANIMALS

WILD ANIMALS

Carus Publishing Company

1/07